DINOSAUR PROFILES

PLATEOSAURUS

Titles in the Dinosaur Profiles series include:

Ankylosaurus

Diplodocus

Giganotosaurus

Iguanodon

Ornitholestes

Pachycephalosaurus

Plateosaurus

Velociraptor

DINOSAUR PROFILES

PLATEOSAURUS

Text by Fabio Marco Dalla Vecchia
Illustrations by Leonello Calvetti and Luca Massini

BLACKBIRCH PRESS

An imprint of Thomson Gale, a part of The Thomson Corporation

THOMSON

GALE

Detroit • New York • San Francisco • New Haven, Conn. • Waterville, Maine • London

Computer illustrations 3D and 2D: Leonello Calvetti and Luca Massini

Photographs: page 21, Fabio Marco Dalla Vecchia

LIBRARY OF CONGRESS CATALOGING-IN-PUBLICATION DATA

Dalla Vecchia, Fabio Marco.
Plateosaurus / text by Fabio Marco Dalla Vecchia ; illustrations by Leonello Calvetti and Luca Massini.
    p. cm.—(Dinosaur profiles)
Includes bibliographical references and index.
ISBN-13: 978-1-4103-0744-6 (hardcover)
ISBN-10: 1-4103-0744-1 (hardcover)
1. Plateosaurus—Juvenile literature. 2. Dinosaurs—Evolution—Juvenile literature.
I. Calvetti, Leonello, ill. II. Massini, Luca, ill. III. Title.

QE862.S3D398 2007
567.913--dc22

2007001517

Printed in the United States of America
10 9 8 7 6 5 4 3 2 1

Contents

A Changing World 6

A Gentle Plant Eater 8

Babies 10

Food 13

An Easy Life 15

Dangerous Waters 17

The Plateosaurus Body 18

Digging Up Plateosaurus 20

Protosauropods 23

The Evolution of Dinosaurs 24

A Dinosaur's Family Tree 26

Glossary 28

For More Information 29

About the Author 30

Index 31

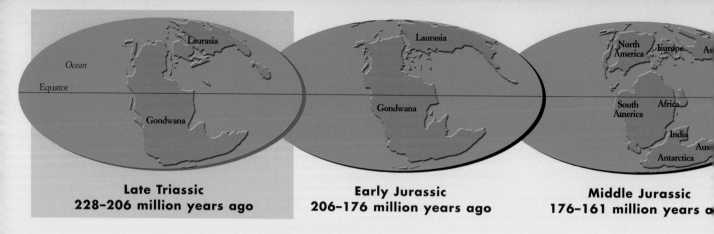

Late Triassic
228–206 million years ago

Early Jurassic
206–176 million years ago

Middle Jurassic
176–161 million years a

A Changing World

Earth's long history began 4.6 billion years ago. Dinosaurs are some of the most fascinating animals from the planet's long past.

The word *dinosaur* comes from the word *dinosauria*. This word was invented by the English scientist Richard Owen in 1842. It comes from two Greek words, *deinos* and *sauros*. Together, these words mean "terrifying lizards."

The dinosaur era, also called the Mesozoic era, lasted from 228 million years ago to 65 million years ago. It is divided into three periods. The first, the Triassic period, lasted about 42 million years. The second, the Jurassic period, lasted 61 million years. The third, the Cretaceous period, lasted about 79 million years. Dinosaurs ruled the world for a huge time span of 160 million years.

Like dinosaurs, mammals appeared at the end of the Triassic period. During the time of dinosaurs, mammals were small animals the size of a mouse. Only after dinosaurs became extinct did mammals develop into the many forms that exist today.

Late Jurassic
1–144 million years ago

Early Cretaceous
144–100 million years ago

Late Cretaceous
100–65 million years ago

Humans never met Mesozoic dinosaurs. The dinosaurs were gone nearly 65 million years before humans appeared on Earth.

Dinosaurs changed in time. Stegosaurus and Brachiosaurus no longer existed when Tyrannosaurus and Triceratops appeared 75 million years later.

The dinosaur world was different from today's world. The climate was warmer, with few extremes. The position of the continents was different. Plants were constantly changing, and grass did not even exist.

A Gentle Plant Eater

Plateosaurus was the most common dinosaur of its time. It lived during the late Triassic and early Jurassic periods, between 225 and 180 million years ago. It belonged to a family of dinosaurs known as prosauropods. The prosauropods were closely related to the giant sauropods that spread over the Earth during the Jurassic and Cretaceous periods.

Plateosaurus lived in what is today Germany, Switzerland, France, and Greenland. Like all prosauropods, Plateosaurus had a small head, a huge, barrel-shaped body, and a slender tail and neck. These dinosaurs could grow up to 30 feet (9m) long and weigh 4 tons (3.6 metric tons). Some were much bigger than others. For that reason, scientists believe that males and females were different sizes.

The name *Plateosaurus* means "flat lizard." The man who gave the dinosaur this name never explained why he did so. It might have been because he thought some parts of the skeleton looked flat.

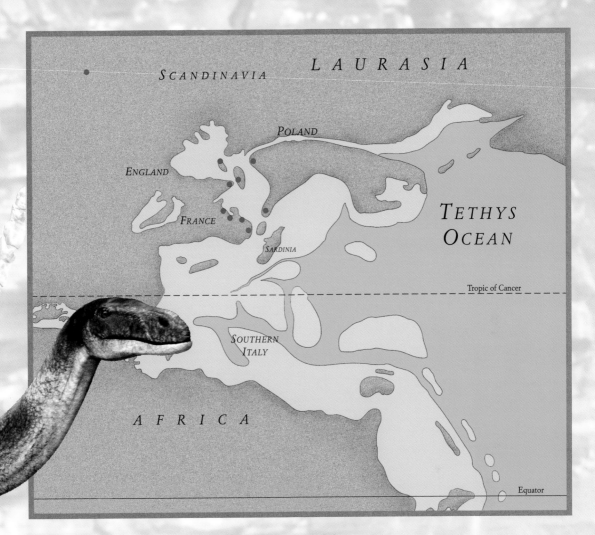

This map shows what is today northern Europe and the Mediterranean Sea during the late Triassic period. The darker blue areas show deep waters, and the lighter blue areas show shallow waters. The red dots mark places where Plateosaurus fossils have been discovered.

BABIES

Paleontologists (scientists who study dinosaurs) have not discovered any Plateosaurus nests or eggs. But they have found the eggs and nests of Mussaurus, a close relative. Tiny skeletons of newly hatched Mussaurus have also been found. They are so small that they could fit in a person's hand.

The name *Mussaurus* means "lizard mouse," which is what the newly hatched creatures looked like. They had large heads and enormous eyes. Sometimes the babies were preyed upon by small meat-eating dinosaurs.

Food

The plateosaurs had teeth shaped like those of modern iguana lizards. For that reason, scientists believe that they ate mostly plants. Their favorite foods were probably tender leaves, fruits, and buds. They may have occasionally eaten small animals or scavenged on dead ones. As the young plateosaurs grew, they could browse on leaves that were several feet from the ground and thus out of reach of other plant-eating animals.

An Easy Life

Plateosaurus lived near ponds and lakes, where many tropical plants grew. Its neighbor was Proganochelys, the earliest known turtle. Plateosaurus could eat in safety, because few meat-eating dinosaurs preyed on it.

Dangerous Waters

Plateosaurus lived in areas where there were many shallow, muddy lakes. Plateosaurs that made their way into these ponds alone or in groups often sank into the mud because of their weight. If they were unable to free themselves, they starved to death. This gave small, light theropods, the main predators of the time, plenty of food.

THE PLATEOSAURUS BODY

Plateosaurus was a huge animal. Its neck was long, which allowed it to browse on leaves high up in trees. Its head was small compared to its body. In its jaws were 27 to 35 small, leaf-shaped teeth with jagged edges. Because its front limbs were long and strong, Plateosaurus probably moved around mostly on four legs. But it did occasionally stand only on its hind limbs.

Each hand on the front limbs had three strong claws. These were used to dig and to tear food. The claws might also have been used for defense against predators. The back feet had four clawed toes and a fifth short, stubby toe.

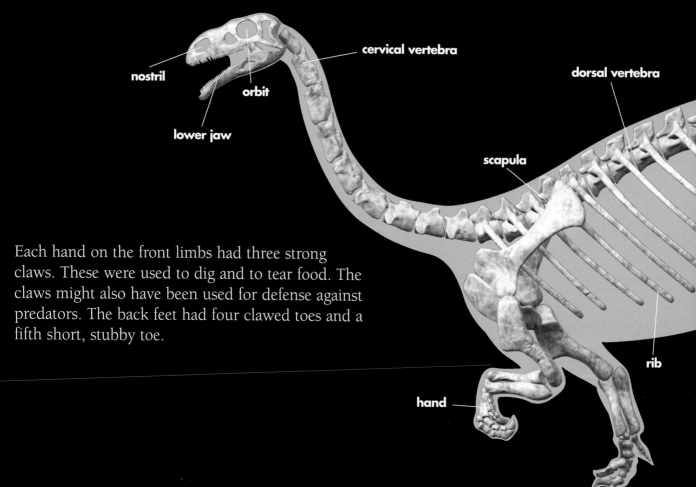

nostril

orbit

lower jaw

cervical vertebra

dorsal vertebra

scapula

rib

hand

Side view of the skull

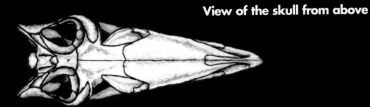

View of the skull from above

Lower jaw bones

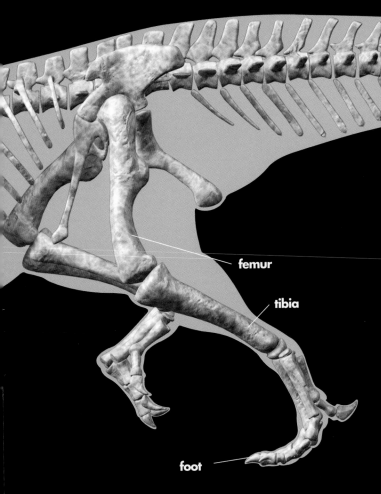

caudal vertebra

femur

tibia

foot

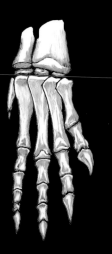

Bones and claws of the back foot

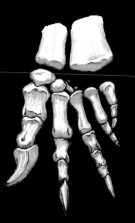

Bones and claws of the front foot

19

Digging Up Plateosaurus

In 1906, a young student stumbled across a large number of Plateosaurus bones in southern Germany. German paleontologists who dug at the site uncovered more than 50 skeletons. Many of these were complete. Later, groups of skeletons were discovered at other sites in Germany as well. In these areas, plateosaurs were trapped in mud, and their remains collected year after year.

Because so many complete Plateosaurus skeletons have been found, it is one of the best known dinosaurs. It was also one of the first dinosaurs to be given a scientific name. German paleontologist Herbert von Mayer named it in 1837.

Many Plateosaurus skeletons are on display at the National Museum of Natural History in Stuttgart, Germany. A skeleton is also on display in the American Museum of Natural History in New York City.

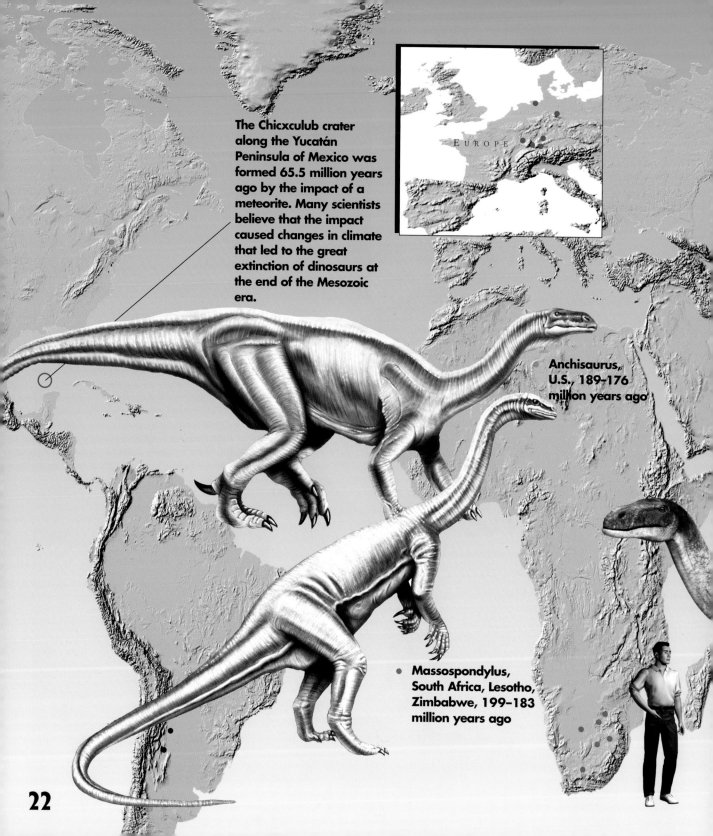

The Chicxculub crater along the Yucatán Peninsula of Mexico was formed 65.5 million years ago by the impact of a meteorite. Many scientists believe that the impact caused changes in climate that led to the great extinction of dinosaurs at the end of the Mesozoic era.

EUROPE

Anchisaurus, U.S., 189–176 million years ago

Massospondylus, South Africa, Lesotho, Zimbabwe, 199–183 million years ago

PROTOSAUROPODS

opposite: This map shows sites where the protosauropods pictured below have been found.

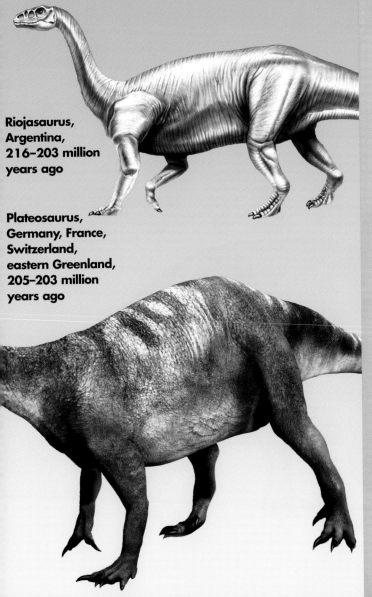

Riojasaurus, Argentina, 216–203 million years ago

Plateosaurus, Germany, France, Switzerland, eastern Greenland, 205–203 million years ago

THE GREAT EXTINCTION

Sixty-five million years ago, 140 million years after the time of Plateosaurus, dinosaurs became extinct. This may have happened because a large meteorite struck earth. A wide crater caused by a meteorite 65 million years ago has been located along the coast of the Yucatán Peninsula in Mexico. The impact of the meteorite would have produced an enormous amount of dust. This dust would have stayed suspended in the atmosphere and blocked sunlight for a long time. A lack of sunlight would have caused a drastic drop in the earth's temperature and killed plants. The plant-eating dinosaurs would have died, starved and frozen. As a result, meat-eating dinosaurs would have had no prey and would also have starved.

Some scientists believe dinosaurs did not die out completely. They think that birds were feathered dinosaurs that survived the great extinction. That would make the present-day chicken and all of its feathered relatives descendants of the large dinosaurs.

THE EVOLUTION OF DINOSAURS

The oldest dinosaur fossils are 220–225 million years old and have been found mainly in South America. They have also been found in Africa, India, and North America. Dinosaurs probably evolved from small and nimble bipedal reptiles like the Triassic Lagosuchus of Argentina. Dinosaurs were able to rule the world because their legs were held directly under the body, like those of modern mammals. This made them faster and less clumsy than other reptiles.

Since 1887, dinosaurs have been divided into two groups based on the structure of their hips. Saurischian dinosaurs had hips shaped like those of modern lizards. Ornithischian dinosaurs had hips shaped like those of modern birds.

Triceratops is one of the ornithischian dinosaurs, whose hip bones (inset) are shaped like those of modern birds.

Tyrannosaurus is in the saurischian group of dinosaurs, whose hip bones (inset) are shaped like those of modern lizards.

There are two main groups of saurischians. One group is sauropodomorphs. This group includes sauropods, such as Brachiosaurus. Sauropods ate plants and were quadrupedal, meaning they walked on four legs. The other group of saurischians, theropods, includes bipedal meat-eating predators. Some paleontologists believe birds are a branch of theropod dinosaurs.

Ornithischians are all plant eaters. They are divided into three groups. Thyreophorans include the quadrupedal stegosaurians, including Stegosaurus, and ankylosaurians, including Ankylosaurus. The other two groups are ornithopods, which includes Edmontosaurus and marginocephalians.

A Dinosaur's Family Tree

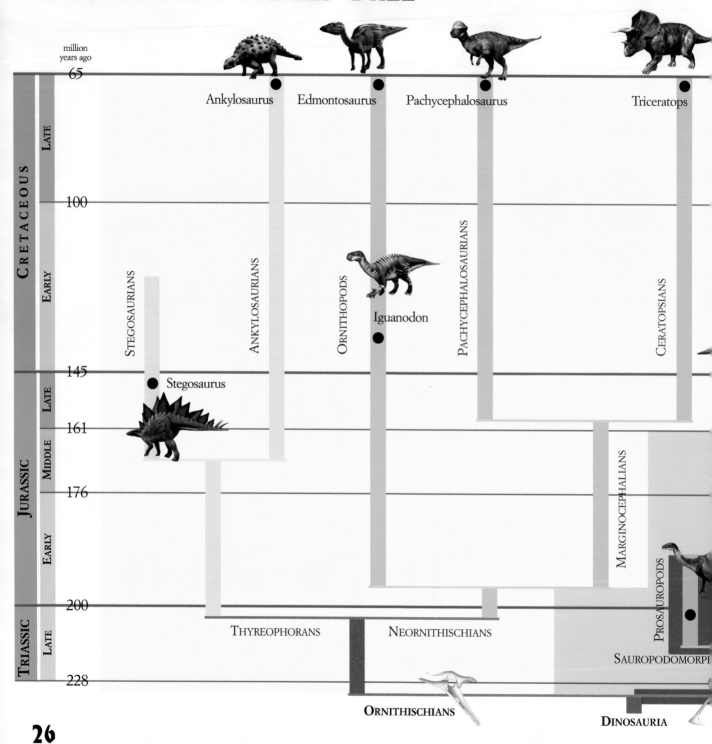

million years ago

65

100

145

161

176

200

228

CRETACEOUS — LATE, EARLY

JURASSIC — LATE, MIDDLE, EARLY

TRIASSIC — LATE

Ankylosaurus

Edmontosaurus

Pachycephalosaurus

Triceratops

STEGOSAURIANS

ANKYLOSAURIANS

ORNITHOPODS

Iguanodon

PACHYCEPHALOSAURIANS

CERATOPSIANS

Stegosaurus

MARGINOCEPHALIANS

PROSAUROPODS

THYREOPHORANS

NEORNITHISCHIANS

SAUROPODOMORPH

ORNITHISCHIANS

DINOSAURIA

Ornithomimus

Tyrannosaurus

Velociraptor

ORNITHOMIMOIDEANS

TYRANNOSAUROIDS

OVIRAPTOROSAURIANS

DEINONYCHOSAURIANS

BIRDS

Giganotosaurus

Deinonychus

Scipionyx

Caudipteryx

SAUROPODS

urus   Diplodocus

Ornitholestes

THEROPODS

us

SAURISCHIANS

Glossary

Bipedal moving on two feet

Caudal related to the tail

Cervical related to the neck

Claws sharp, pointed nails on the fingers and toes of predators

Cretaceous period the period of geological time between 144 and 65 million years ago

Dorsal related to the back

Evolution changes in living things over time

Femur thigh bone

Fossil part of a living thing, such as a skeleton or leaf imprint, that has been preserved in Earth's crust from an earlier geological age

Jurassic period the period of geological time between 206 and 144 million years ago

Mesozoic era the period of geological time between 248 and 65 million years ago

Meteorite a piece of iron or rock that falls to Earth from space

Orbit the opening in the skull surrounding the eye

Paleontologist a scientist who studies prehistoric life

Predator an animal that hunts other animals for food

Prey an animal that is hunted by other animals for food

Quadrupedal moving on four feet

Skeleton the structure of an animal body, made up of bones

Skull the bones that form the head and face

Tibia shinbone

Triassic period the period of geological time between 248 and 206 million years ago

Vertebra a bone of the spine

For More Information

Books

Michael Benton and Lynne Gibbs, *The Great Book of Dinosaurs*. London: Chrysalis, 2003.

Dougal Dixon, *Plateosaurus and Other Desert Dinosaurs*. Bloomington, MN: Picture Window Books, 2004.

Virginia Schomp, *Plateosaurus and Other Early Long-Necked Plant-Eaters*. New York: Benchmark Books/Marshall Cavendish, 2006.

Web Sites

Fossil Halls
http://www.amnh.org/exhibitions/permanent/fossilhalls/?src=e_h
This section of the Web page of the American Museum of Natural History provides detailed information about the museum's dinosaur exhibits.

Prehistoric Life
http://www.bbc.co.uk/sn/prehistoric_life/
This section of the BBC Web site contains a great deal of information about dinosaurs, including galleries of illustrations along with games and quizzes.

The Smithsonian National Museum of Natural History
http://www.nmnh.si.edu/paleo/dino/
A virtual tour of the Smithsonian's National Museum of Natural History dinosaur exhibits.

About the Author

Fabio Marco Dalla Vecchia is the curator of the Paleontological Museum of Monfalcone in Gorizia, Italy. He has participated in several paleontological field works in Italy and other countries and has directed paleontological excavations in Italy. He is the author of more than 50 scientific articles that have been published in national and international journals.

INDEX

ankylosaurians, 25

babies, 10
bipedal dinosaurs, 25
birds, 23, 25
body, 8, 10, 18
Brachiosaurus, 7, 25

claws, 18
climate, 7, 23
Cretaceous period, 6, 8

dangers, 15, 17
dinosaurs, 6–7
dinosaurs' names, 6, 8

evolution, 7, 23–24
extinction, 7, 23

flat lizards, 8
food, 13
fossils, 10, 20, 24

Germany, 20

Jurassic period, 6, 8

living areas, 15, 17
lizard mouse, 10

mammals, 6
Mesozoic era, 6
meteorite impact, 23
movement, 18, 24
Mussaurus, 10

ornithischians, 24, 25

INDEX

Owen, Richard, 6

plants, 7, 13, 23
predators, 15, 17
Proganochelys, 15
prosauropods, 8

quadrepedal dinosaurs, 25

range, 8

saurischians, 24, 25
sauropodomorphs, 25
sauropods, 25

size, 8
skeletons, 10, 20, 24
Stegosaurus, 7, 25

teeth, 13
terrifying lizards, 6
theropods, 17, 25
thyreophorans, 25
Triassic period, 6, 8
Triceratops, 7
Tyrannosaurus, 7
turtles, 15

von Mayer, Herbert, 20